A PRACTICAL APPROACH

IN LITERATURE REVIEW

Dr. Charudatta Achyut Gandhe

CONTENTS

Chapter 5: Searching the Literature   **41**

PREFACE

We, as a researcher conduct a research to seek a solution for a problem that we are facing. Research is a designed and methodological journey with logical meaning. But how to get a logical meaning to your research? Which method and design will you choose to start your research journey? To get the answers of these question, you try to digging a huge mountain of literature in respective area. Everything you get from this may not be useful, may not be practical, may not be directly related to your research, but you will definitely get an overall insight to your research journey. The literature review keeps you engaged with the critical thinking about past research related to your own research in hand. It tries to establish the linkage between the efforts taken in past and efforts to be taken in future. This is literature review. We often says that literature review finds a research gap, of course it helps you to find research gaps, but in more ways, it gives you motivation, it gives you solutions, it helps you get rid of impossible situation occurred due to several circumstances, it supports you and overall it is the hidden research guide who tries to guide you through your entire research journey along with your guide. It helps you to develop your research or scholarly voice. It develops your understanding about topic.

Research is a systematic and a continuous process that includes defining you topic, choosing an appropriate design, selection of an appropriate sample, developing research tool, choosing appropriate and relevant statistical techniques. Superficially, these are different process, but these are interlinked with each other. Many times, it is noticed that researcher writes a plan of research which contains all these processes but lacking of a main part i.e. literature review. Or just write "for literature review, researcher will search research databases, journals and books". In an ideal situation, after finalizing your research topic, you are supposed to spend a sufficient amount of time to read the literature related to your topic and then supposed to finalize rest of the things. A research based on a strong, comprehensive and relevant literature always proves it suitable so as to give solution to the problem.

In this sense, there are many misconceptions about literature review. How much literature should I read? What type of literature should I read? Shall I supposed to read literature published on national or international level? How long should I keep myself busy in literature review process? Shall I include only doctoral Thesis or journal articles also? Shall I refer websites or blogs? How should I write literature review? How many pages should I write literature review? Is there any standard process or method to write literature review? And so on.

This books intends to give the answers to all these and similar questions. Literature review is the most important as well as generally neglected part of research. So this book also focuses on its importance, methodology of writing the systematic review which could be a kind of value addition to your research. This books is divided in three parts. First part will cover the theoretical aspects of literature review i.e. concept, need, importance and types of literature reviews. Second part will cover the searching of literature. i.e. various sources and resources in library, conventional and non-conventional sources of information, various online research databases. This part will also focus on search strategy and various search techniques to search literature from internet. Third part will cover the reading of literature i.e. how to read and what to read from literature and writing of literature review i.e. the method and procedure of writing literature review.

As a researcher and author of this book I am pretty much sure about the contribution of this book throughout your research journey.

Wish you a happy (RESEARCH) Journey!!!!!!

Dr Charudatta Gandhe

PART

1

CHAPTER 1
THEORETICAL ASPECTS OF LITERATURE REVIEW

What is meant by Literature in Research?

Being a librarian, often a question is asked that, I want thesis on this particular area. If I say we don't have a thesis on this area in our library, the research sitting next to me then asked that how can I write literature review. According to this novice researcher, M.Phil and Ph.D theses are the only source for literature review. Many thesis also have the only listing of M.Phil and Ph.D thesis with some commentary. This is because, he is having a misconception about the literature i.e. he only knows that research means M.Phil. and Ph.D. and thesis means a tool to refer those research. He doesn't know the other literature that comes under the category of "Research". So when you think about literature in research it means not only research done for M.Phil and Ph.D, but it can be a journal article at local, state, national or international level, it can be any research project funded by any organization, it can be an instructional project, it can be a collaborative research project. All these literature is collectively called as scholarly literature. Scholarly literature means nothing but the literature revealed from research. There should not be any language or geographical barrier for literature. Though your research is limited up to your own college students, you can search the literature at international level so as to comprehend what has been done with respect to draw a solution for the similar problem. This will widen your perspective towards the research area. So firstly, we need to remove a misconception that for literature review, we need to refer only M.Phil and Ph.D thesis and no other. Any kind of research, carried at any level without any geographical boundaries could be a treated as literature to be reviewed.

Secondly for theoretical review we need to study the theories established before. This will help you to design a theoretical framework for your research. Besides books and encyclopedias, essays by experts, critics on theories, blogs of experts in the field, newspaper clippings, academic websites would also help in developing your theoretical understanding related to your research area.

A Literature Means:

- P.G., M.Phil and Ph.D Dissertations and Thesis
- Research articles published in any state, national or international journal.
- Research articles published in journals that are indexed in various research databases.
- Research project funded by any academic or commercial organization.
- *Academic Essays, writings, communications.*
- *Theoretical aspects covered in Reference Books and Encyclopedias.*
- *Newspaper clippings related to research area.*
- *Historical Reference sources related to research area.*
- *Authorized and reliable websites, blogs and wikis related to research area.*

After understanding the range of literature that we need to search, one very important thing to be remembered is that we must search a literature telling facts and not the fictions. Secondly, the literature should be align with your research area. It should support or guide you and not divert you. The Literature should not be biased or opinion makers. It should have certain research base and should be written and organized logically. Proper justification should be given wherever necessary. The literature must be published in reliable publications following necessary standards. The literature which has its own citation and having references should be considered as reliable literature for research. You are supposed to collect literature that covers all the dimensions of your research, increase your understanding about your research area, clears and widens your perspective towards research itself and your research area, answers your doubts, makes you to think critically, shows and leads you further towards successful progression of your research is the reliable literature for any research.

What is means by Literature Review?

Literature review is said to be an inherent part of any research. Because without literature review, you can not comprehend various aspects of the topic, without this comprehension you can not proceed to actual research process. With the literature review a researcher can sail in the ocean of literature related to his research topic. Based on this sailing, he plans his further research journey. In simple words, it can be said that literature review is an initial as well as an essential part of any research which helps you to understand various dimensions and past research related to your topic.

Fink (2005) defined literature review as "a systematic, explicit, and reproducible method for identifying, evaluating, and synthesizing the existing body of completed and recorded work produced by researchers, scholars, and practitioners." Fink focuses on the word "systematic". He may think that review should be organized with logical interpretation of yours. Proper justifications should be given and should be expressed in explicit words.

One misconception, which was written before also, literature review is not only mere listing of past research with superficial commentary and at the end written the difference between past research and your research. This practice is mainly observed in social science research. No theoretical plot is created, no arguments, no judgements, no logical A literature review is a list of books and journal articles on a specific topic grouped by theme and **evaluated with regard to your research.** (Moll-Willard, Elizabeth, 2018). This the listing of literature or literature report and not the literature review. It is an evidence of an academic writing aims at demonstrating the deep understanding of the literature available in academic resources on a topic in hand. It mainly contains two internal parts. First part contains the review of various methods, theories, evidences etc and in the second part the criticism is written in the light of the present scenario. It leads us to understand that there could be many or diverse solutions to the same problem depending upon certain circumstances including population, time and method used.

Bem (1995) stated that many authors of literature reviews He stressed on the evidence based review and also systematic review returns you the best evidence from all the evidence

There is also some confusion between two terms i.e. literature review and research synthesis. Are these two terms different or the same? Though these are two different terms, the research synthesis is the part of literature review itself. We first identify and select the studies related to our topic, and then the results of these studies are analyzed and summarized and synthesized. We accessed different studies with different methods, different populations, and different research tools and even with different findings. But all these studies are analyzed from our research point of view. So after analyzing, it is summarized and then synthesized like a continuous story either chronologically or categorically. So synthesizing is the step after analyzing the studies and before reviewing the studies in whole. After synthesizing, we come to know what methods have been used for varied objectives, whether separate, need-based research tools have been developed or used available standard research tools, which statistical techniques have been used and in what circumstances, did sample cover the entire population and whether the findings are consistent across multiple studies. Are the previous researchers agreed or disagreed upon past studies or new theories have been established after certain studies. You can get answers to all these questions after the synthesis. In simple words, synthesis is nothing but joining independent pieces in the form of previous studies into one large and continuous story of efforts taken in past related to your topic.

Why Literature Review?

We have discussed earlier that literature review is an inherent part of any research. Without literature review no research is said to be completed. Literature review is equally important as research method, objectives, sample, research tool and of course findings. Besides that, for clarity, we can list out the reasons why literature review is important in research point of view and researcher point of view. At the same time, the research and researcher both the enriching with the process of literature review.

From Research Point of View:

- It develops a theoretical framework of your research.

- It provides the arguments with logical justification about past studies.

- It shows new ways to interpret.

- It identifies the gaps between past research and current situation.

- It identifies the chronological development in the field.

- It identifies the past errors to avoid in future.

- It validates the originality of research.

- It shows the controversies among the arguments in the field.

- It reveals any gap in the literature.

- It shows different expressions and interpretations about the same idea.

From Researcher Point of view:

- It demonstrates your understanding with the research topic.

- It helps to position yourself in relation to other researcher in the field.

- It motivates and supports you to carry your research.

- It makes you aware of various circumstances in which the problems are addressed in past.

- It supports you to use new methods, models, standards, policies, reports which have been used and/or tested in past research.

- It forces you to motivate critically.

- It develops your Scholarly Voice.

- You get aware of various ways or efforts to solve a particular problem.

- It makes you to think out of the box.

- It makes you to think out of the box.

- It pushes you towards a deep understanding of the topic by considering all the dimensions.

- It introduces you to new stories that motivate you.

It is not one of the chapters in your thesis or dissertation, but it is the base of your research and demonstrates your efforts in searching, reading, comprehending, augmenting, justifying and applying it in the context of your research.

CHAPTER 2

TYPES OF LITERATURE REVIEW

In all six types of literature review are in existence, Namely

1. Traditional Literature Review

2. Scoping Review

3. Systematic Review

4. Annotated Bibliography

5. Standalone Literature Review

6. Integrative Literature Review

1. Traditional or Narrative Literature Review

It is also called as narrative literature review. According to Baker (2016), a traditional review also called narrative literature review. It criticizes and analyses current knowledge on a topic comprehensively and objectively. It is mainly written in the context of your research and is an essential part of it. It helps to develop theoretical framework in the contest of your research. It helps you to find the gap/s in the knowledge.

Onwuegbuzie and Frels (2016) defined four types of narrative reviews:

1. **General literature review** covers the critical analysis of various aspects of current knowledge

on the topic. It is in the form of introduction to the thesis or dissertation. Moreover, it must be defined by research objective and should contain hypothesis

2. **Theoretical literature review** tries to establish the connection between theory and current research.

3. **Methodological literature review** stress upon the method and designs used for current research. It critically analyzes the strengths and weaknesses of the methods and designs along with future directions.

4. **Historical literature review** historical development or journey of a topic. It starts when the issue/topic was address first time and analyzes the journey of the issue/topic till date. The purpose is to place research in a historical context to show familiarity with state-of-the- art developments and to identify the likely directions for future research.

Following are few examples of traditional or narrative literature review.

-   Johnston, B., & Webber, S. (2003). Information literacy in higher education: a review and case study. Studies in higher education, 28(3), 335-352.

-   Hoyles, C. (1992). Mathematics teaching and mathematics teachers: A meta-case study. For the learning of mathematics, 12(3), 32-44.

2. Scoping Review

It is related to identifying the existing literature on a specific research question.

Munn et al., 2018, says that "scoping reviews stress upon showcasing the map of evidence rather than to critical approsal of results. Scoping Reviews are nevertheless "systematic-like", and require a rigorous approach. Scoping review demands the systematic and fairly exhaustive searching. They often include a protocol; the searching is systematic and fairly exhaustive; and methods are documented thoroughly. Scoping review acts as a forerunner to a full systematic review.

Following are some examples of scoping reviews.

- Tricco, A. C., Lillie, E., Zarin, W., O"brien, K., Colquhoun, H., Kastner, M., ... & Straus, S. E. (2016). A scoping review on the conduct and reporting of scoping reviews. BMC medical research methodology, 16, 1-10.

- Pham, M. T., Rajić, A., Greig, J. D., Sargeant, J. M., Papadopoulos, A., & McEwen, S. A. (2014). A scoping review of scoping reviews: advancing the approach and enhancing the consistency. Research synthesis methods, 5(4), 371-385.

3. Systematic Literature Review

Systematic literature is originated in medicines and follows evidence based practice. Dewey, A and Drahota, A (2016) defined a systematic literature review as " the review that identifies, selects and critically appraises research in order to answer a clearly formulated question." The systematic literature review is predefined protocol and preplanned also. Multiple research databases are supposed to searched comprehensively. This type of literature review also stressed upon studying of gray literature like reports, policies, newsletter, government documents etc. It demands the comprehensive and multidimensional search with predefined search strategy. While writing literature review it is supposed to write search strategy, search techniques etc. Pittway (2008) outlines seven key principles behind systematic literature reviews

- Transparency
- Clarity
- Integration
- Focus
- Equality
- Accessibility
- Coverage

In short we can say that systematic literature review gives answers to predefined questions along with evidences where and how these answers are collected. It demands transparency and clarity.

Following are few examples of systematic review.

- Koufogiannakis, D., & Wiebe, N. (2006). Effective methods for teaching information literacy skills to undergraduate students: A systematic review and meta-analysis. Library and Information Science: Parameters and Perspectives, 3(3), 3-43

- Dyment, J. E., & Downing, J. J. (2020). Online initial teacher education: A systematic review of the literature. Asia-Pacific Journal of Teacher Education, 48(3), 316-333.

4. Annotated Bibliography

It is a list of citation to book, articles and documents. Each citation is written along with its brief description and evaluation. Annotations are brief, description and mainly involved critics about the content and author's viewpoints. It gives a clear idea about the particular literature by its annotation.

It is not compulsory to refer all the sources i.e. books, Journals or document or any one. You can write an annotated bibliography only on journal articles also. You can define a time range also i.e. annotated bibliography related to ABC area, it will cover only journal articles published during 2010 to 2023. It can be extended on the scope of research or an assignment. It could be given as a basic assignment before starting actual research or can be given to novice researchers go get the superficial idea about the body of knowledge in that specific field. Annotated bibliography could be useful, if taken before planning and conducting comprehensive literature review. Following are few examples of annotated bibliography.

- Tacon, A. G., Coelho, R. T., Levy, J., Machado, T. M., Neiva, C. R., & Lemos, D. (2023). Annotated Bibliography of Selected Papers Dealing with the Health Benefits and Risks of Fish and Seafood Consumption. Reviews in Fisheries Science & Aquaculture, 1- 95.

- Brodeur, K., Crampton, A., Faase, C., Israelson, M., Madison, S. M., O"Byrne, W. I., & Sulzer, M.

(2023). Annotated Bibliography of Research in the Teaching of English. Research in the Teaching of English, 57(3), AB1-AB46.

5. Standalone Literature Review

It is also called as simple literature review. It not a part of any large research. It is a critics in the form of document that reviews relevant documents on a particular topic. It is written logically in the context of a topic. Like annotated bibliography, it could be given as an independent assignment to students or novice researcher. It is supposed to search, access, summarize, analyze and synthesize the literature for understanding the current situation of a particular topic. It does not require to write or mention search strategy like systematic literature review. It is just useful to get the topic clearly understood. It summarizes what the literature says related to this topic.

It is not argumentative, rather it supports the arguments that you made before conducting this type of review. Unlike the review as part of any research, this type of literature review does not intend to find the gaps. It could be useful by experts and professionals for keeping the updating. Following are few examples of standalone literature review.

6. Integrative Literature Review

According to Broome (1993), an integrative review is a specific review method that summarizes past empirical or theoretical literature to provide a greater comprehensive understanding of a particular phenomenon or healthcare problem. It does not review the primary literature or primary review, but also other secondary or non-research documents such as reports, policies, opinions, discussion papers etc.

According to Toronto, C., & Remington, R.(2020), Whitmore et al. (2005), Broome (1993): an integrative review approach is best suited for:

- A research scope focused more broadly at a phenomenon of interest rather than a systematic review and allows for diverse research, which may contain theoretical and methodological literature to address the aim of the review

- Supporting a wide range of inquiry, such as defining concepts, reviewing theories, or analyzing methodological issues

- Examining the complexity of nursing practice more broadly by using diverse data sources The aim of this review is to

- Define a concept, review theories, review evidences and analyzes methodological issues.

The strength of an ILR lies in summarizing the findings of multiple types of evidence addressing a problem and could, therefore, be the preferred type of review in a clinical setting to provide a more inclusive view of a topic informing practice (Cowell, 2015).

CHAPTER 3

PLANNING A LITERATURE REVIEW

Researcher always ask that when shall I start the literature review? How much literature should I supposed to collect? How Many pages long should be the literature review? Just ask a question to yourself. When you start the research? The answer is you start the research when you encounter any problem and you try to find its solution. This clearly means that your literature review should start immediately after you encounter a problem so as to search, if there is any similar problem and its solution reported in literature. Literature Review is a process to be started well before starting your actual research. Before defining your objectives, method, scope, you are supposed to search for the literature based on your research questions. Means when you encounter any problem, you should transform it into research question/s ,and then try to search the literature where similar problems / research questions and its solutions are reported, then access that literature, analyze it, synthesize it and then review it. After reviewing the literature, you will be able to find the research gap. So it's a continuous process starting from defining or formulating research questions.

Consider a scenario. You have invited 6 guests at your home for a dinner. This guests includes, old aged, mid aged, younger and kids. So, will you cook the food without thinking with the available material in the kitchen or will you plan a special dinner for guests? Obviously, you will plan a special dinner for it. Now you start thinking. Who are my guests? Accordingly I need to decide my menu so that it could be suited to all aged guests. After finalizing the menu, you will make a list of required items to cook the menu. After making list, you come to know that, some of the items in the lists are available and rest you need to purchase from market. You check the available items once whether it is in good condition or not and if not, accordingly you correct the list. And then you go to market. In market, you need to visit different types of shops, or in a mall, different counters or sections to purchase the items in list as all are not of same type. After checking, reviewing the each item, if not liked, you visit another shop and then purchase it. After coming back to home, you recall the recipe of the dish to be cooked, and accordingly as per the recipe, you use the items in an original or in required or in altered form. You cook the dish and serve to guest. And you get much satisfied when guests appreciates your cooked dish.

Now relate the process of literature review with the above scenario. Following table explains the similarities between this scenario and literature review.

Description in Scenario	Literature Review
Invited guests (included old aged, mid aged, younger and kids)	Planning a research on specific area
Deciding for a dish to be cooked	Defining objectives and formulating research question

Description in Scenario	Literature Review
Listing all the items required to cook the dish	Identifying the dimensions of research based on objectives and research questions.
Checking the availability of any of the items in kitchen	Checking the availability of literature at library.
Modify the list accordingly	Modifying the dimensions
Visit different shops as per the item	Searching multiple databases, libraries, ETDs, etc. for literature according to identified dimensions
Check, test and then purchase	Access, evaluate, analyze, synthesis the literature
Recall the recipe	Revisit the objectives and research questions
Use the items in original or required form for the dish	Read , comprehend and criticize the literature from your research point of view
Cook the dish	Write a review

As for any type of research, a literature review should be planned and managed as project (Lyratzopoulos and Allen, 2004). Booth.et.al (2012) suggested that, as for any project, the reviewer, or review, or review team, needs to consider the elements of time, quality, and money.

Balancing these three considerations within an agreed timescale for delivery, whether one year for a dissertation or thesis or a longer period of time for a commissioned project, is a key to the success of a literature review. You are supposed to allocate sufficient time for literature review. Based on the above discussion, actually literature review is an end product, to reach to an end product, you are supposed to travel through following steps:

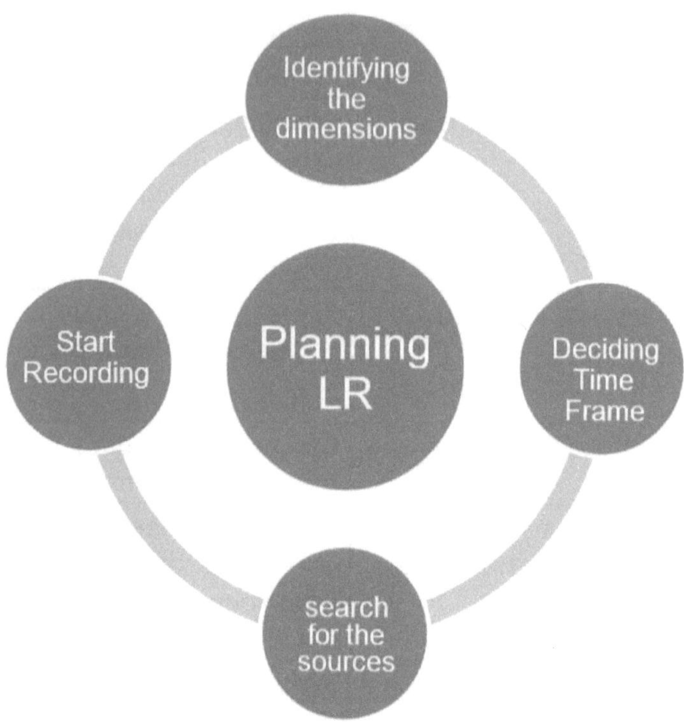

Identify Dimensions

If you think anything as a whole, it is quite difficult rather than think the same thing in parts and then into whole. Likewise, if you think your topic without considering its dimensions, it will be difficult or some of its dimensions could be missed out. So splitting your topic in various dimensions is important so that you can think clearly. This is explained with following example.

Title of the Research.: Developing an Information Literacy Programme for students of Pre-service Teacher Education: An Experimental Research.

From above title it gets clear that the research is related to developing an intervention program for Pre service teacher education students. Based on the topic of research, following dimensions could be identified. According to each dimension, in next step, formulate a question followed by type of document in broad. This is explained in following table

Dimensions	Question to be asked	Broader Type of Document
Information Literacy Definition	What is the definition of Information Literacy?	Theoretical
Information Literacy History/ Development	What is the history/ developmental history of Information Literacy?	Theoretical
Information Literacy Standards	Are there any standards available for Information Literacy, and which?	Theoretical and Research

Dimensions	Question to be asked	Broader Type of Document
Information Literacy Models	Are there any Models available for Information Literacy, and which?	Theoretical and Research
Information Literacy Evaluation	Which evaluation techniques have been used for evaluation information literacy?	Theoretical and Research
Information Literacy Test	Is there any standardize information literacy Test available?	Theoretical and Research
Information Literacy Teaching	Which teaching methods are used for teaching information literacy teaching?	Theoretical and Research
Information Lietracy Learning	Which learning techniques are used for learning information literacy teaching?	Theoretical and Research
Information Literacy Curriculum	Is there any curriculum drafted or available for information literacy?	Theoretical and Research

Dimensions	Question to be asked	Broader Type of Document
Information Literacy Programme	Are there any information literacy program/s available in general?	Theoretical and Research
Information Literacy Programme for Teacher Education	Are there any information literacy program/s available for teacher education?	Theoretical and Research

These dimensions are nothing but the conceptual scope of your literature review. You are supposed to search the literature on each of the dimension given in above table. These dimensions, altogether, will cover the topic comprehensively. If you only search for information literacy programme for pre service teacher education as a whole, you may not get the literature on all its dimensions. So defining a scope or identifying the dimensions of your research and so of your literature review is very important step before starting your literature review.

Deciding Time Frame

We discussed when we should start the literature review. Many researcher ask till when should take review? What should be the time span? Should I review very old literature also or should I limit it since last 20 years? Answer is that , start the literature since when the first research is published in that area and till you complete your research. For example, the term **information**

literacy was coined in 1970s, but the concept was practicing since 19th century. So I need to review the documents since 19th century. I should take a review in chronological order as the concept develops. Number of year is not important, but the research reported in the area should be covered so as to understand the topic and the histprical journey in that topic. All the steps in building the subject should becovered.

Deciding the Sources

As a librarian, I always experience that, many researcher focuses on only M.phil and Ph.D Thesis or dissertations for research physically available in a library. They are not aware of other sources where research is published. For any literature review, you are supposed to consider each research whether it is an unpublished M.Phil or Ph.D Thesis, or an institutional research project or Minor/ Major Research Project, Research Article published in a state, national or international journal despite of it is offline or online or in a journal that is in any online research database. So do not restrict yourself with the thesis and dissertations only and try to dig out the literature from various offline and online sources.

Start Recording

It is usually seen that, many researcher access literature from offline or online resources for their research. But they never record any reference at that time. Later, when they try to access it or try to find it in library, they do not get. In that case they can not cite those resources in their thesis. Online resources are generally volatile, there is not guarantee that you can have access to them anytime in future also. So it is better to record a diary or a file and write down the references of each article you refer, so that you can avoid future inconvenience.

PART

2

CHAPTER 4

RESOURCES FOR LITERATURE

For studying the literature, we are supposed to know from where we can collect it. Many times researchers download it from any website which may not be authorized or reliable. So It is important to know the reliable resource which is available on website. Firstly we should know the basic types of information.

There are two basic types of information sources.

- Primary Information Sources
- Secondary Information Sources

A primary source is a document through which a newly created information is communicated firstly. Examples of primary sources include: Diaries, Letters, Speeches, and Journals, News Papers etc.

A secondary source is document which interprets and analyzes the information in primary sources. Secondary sources may have pictures, quotes or graphics of primary sources in them. Some types of secondary sources include: Text Books, Criticisms, History and encyclopaedia etc.

- Despite of these basic types of information sources, following are various types of information sources.

- Reference Sources
- Non Book Sources
- Electronic Sources
- Periodicals

Reference Sources

Almanac

An **almanac** is an annual publication that includes information regarding weather forecasts, farmers' planting dates, tide tables, and tabular information often arranged according to the calendar. It also contains astronomical data and various statistics such as the daily times of the rising and setting of the sun and moon, eclipses, hours of full tide, stated festivals and so on. A "Date Panchang" is famous almanac published in Marathi Language. Other examples of Almanac is Farmers' Almanac , Schott's Almanac. Almanacs are available in both the forms i.e. printed as well as online. The famous example of Indian online almanac is Kalnirnaya. To collect statistical data in current and past, almanac is the authorized and reliable source.

Year Book

A Year Book is also called as an Annual. A Year Books is a documentary, memorial, or historical book published every year, containing information about the previous year. It is also defined as a usually bound publication compiled by the graduating class of a school or college, recording the year's events and typically containing photographs of students and faculty. Yearbooks are available in both the forms i.e. print and online. A school's annual magazine is an example of yearbook which is familiar to us. Pica boo Year book can help you to discover the ideas of creating school year book. Various universities publish their research yearbook where research in that university in concerned year is recorded.

Handbook

A Handbook is a concise manual or reference book providing specific information or instruction about a subject or place. It is handy reference for carrying out certain task. A Teachers' Handbook is a good example which is available for all school subjects for all standards. Handbook contains the sequence of instructions for performing specific tack e.g. handbook of psychology test or teachers' handbook for teaching geography. Various research handbooks are published on various dimensions at national or international level.

Encyclopaedia

A reference work (often in several volumes) containing articles on various topics (often arranged in alphabetical order) dealing with the entire range of human knowledge or with some particular specialty. An encyclopaedia is an authentic source of information in any subject for back round information. The encyclopedias are mainly of two types. A General Encyclopaedia which covers the general topics in the universe e.g. Encyclopaedia of Britannica or Marathi Vishwakosh. A second types is subject related encyclopaedia which especially covers the nearly all the topics or information from specific subject e.g. Encyclopaedia of Education, Encyclopaedia of Psychology. Due to advent of information technology, the online or digital encyclopaedia in the form of CD are also available. The Encyclopaedia Britannica is also available in CD Rom Format which is more convenient for searching. The Wikipedia is the example of online encyclopaedia which is also interactive.

Encyclopeaedia is the starting point of any research that gives you an authorized background information related to your topic. It helps you to broaden or narrowing you research. It is always the reliable source of information. Now days, encyclopaedias are published in nearly all the disciplines. There are also research encyclopaedias like Encyclopaedia of Research Design by SAGE Publication etc.

Directory

Contains an organized list of specific persons or institutions Private Institutions, Government institutions, social institutions Gives all necessary information about specific persons or institutions Arranged alphabetically. We are all familiar with Telephone directories. Two types of directories are availale. General Directory which directs towards regions, cities, telephone numbers etc. and special directories which directs towards specific organizations, business, education, professionals and professions. As like other reference sources, directories are also available in online form. The Directory of online journals, Web directory, Subject directory are some examples of online directories.

Dictionary: It is a book that lists the words of a language in alphabetical order and gives their meaning, or that gives the equivalent words in a different language. More dictionary provides the pronunciations, various forms of a word. The famous examples of these dictionaries are Oxford Dictionary, Webster's Dictionary for English to English, and Veerker's Dictionary, Navneet Dictionary are multi language dictionary. Other than these dictionary, each language has its own dictionary. As a teacher, especially those who are language teachers, we must know these basic types of dictionaries. The following are the major types of dictionary.

General Dictionary Glossary

Lexicon Thesaurus Concordance

Dictionary of Short forms Dictionary of Usage Dictionary of Technical Terms Dictionary of Quotations Dictionary of Etymology Dictionary of Proverbs Dictionary of Slangs

Non Book Sources:

Non Bok Sources are the sources of information which are not in form of book. A wide range of non book sources is available like charts, maps, gloge, images, drawings, pamphlets, patents, reports, thesis and dissertations, standards. Many of these sources are used in classrooms. But still some sources are ignored though useful.

Letters: We are much familiar with the letters. But we can use the letters for education purposes. Letter are the primary sources of information. You can give reference of letters written by famous people and also can show the copies of these letters in a classroom. For example, Jawaharlal Nehru's Letters to Indira etc. History teachers can make effective use of these letters by showing the historical letters in a classroom.

Diaries: Diaries are the original source of information. The diaries written by famous people are published.

History teachers can make effective use of historical diaries by showing them (in published format) in a classroom.

Pamphlets: We are all familiar with the pamphlets. Many of the pamphlets are produced for marketing purpose. But educational pamphlets are also available which provides the information about various courses, educational schemes.

Electronic Sources

The sources which provided the information in an electronic form are called as electronic sources. To access the information from these sources, we require electronic support. The common examples of these electronic sources are CDs, DVDs, E-journals, E-Books, Televisions, Tape recorders, Cassettes etc. Instead of monotonous teaching from books only, you can use these electronic sources in a classroom which will be definitely useful for expanding the vision of students. For example, if you are teaching a lesson "Eclipses", instead of showing charts or models, if you show them a CD of eclipses, it will be more effective. Same thing is for science teachers, digestive system can be explained more effectively by showing CD, than charts. E- books and E-journals are now emerging very fast. Though it is bit difficult to access it, as a teacher, for knowledge gaining you should refer to these e-journals and e-books as they are available for 24*7 with you.

Periodicals

It is a publication which is published at regular interval such magazine, journal or newspaper. They are also often referred to as serials. Periodicals usually consist of a collection of articles, which may range from a single page story in a magazine to a 40 page study in a scholarly journal.

Advantages of Using Periodicals

- Periodicals are the only best option for current information.

- Before published in a books, the current information, especially research based information, is always first published in a journal.

- Periodicals are the best source for volatile information.

- Periodicals are meant for every field and for every interest.

Many different topics are covered in one periodical.

The most common types of periodicals are **Scholarly**, **Popular**, and **Trade Journals**.

Scholarly Journals

- It contains original research work in a specific field.

- The intended audience is researchers, faculty and students in a specific field.

- The experts and well known personalities in the field write the articles/

- Content is often supported by charts, figures and statistics.

- Do not contains advertisements.

- Articles in a scholarly have to undergone through rigorous peer review process before publications.

- Articles usually include footnotes or bibliographies to other sources, using a standardized citation format.

- Published at State, National or International levels-

As discussed earlier, many researcher think that literature review is only be taken from Ph.D and M.Phil Thesis and Dissertation. However, The scope of literature in terms of research is very vast and could be change according to the topic or research. The following documents could be considered as literature in terms of research.

1. Thesis and Dissertations

2. Research Articles

3. Research Reports

4. Research Abstracts

5. Conference papers and proceedings

6. Reports of various Government and Non-Government Committees

7. Statistical Resources

8. Essays by the authorities or professionals

9. Reference Books

10. Dictionary

Encyclopedia

The list could be altered or extended according to discipline as each discipline has its own protocol to disseminate the information produced. But the resources in the above list could be search independently or it could be available in their respective databases.

E.g. You can search article by accessing individual journal if you not the name of that journal in which that article is published. But, thousands of journal are in existence in various disciplines, so it is difficult to know all the journals in the discipline. So overcome this issue, you can search research databases which holds a number of journals and you can search and access these journals from a single window. So searching research articles through research database could be an easier as well as effective way. EMERALD, SCIENCE DIRECT are the paid research database which holds the journals of variety of disciplines. The databases need to be subscribed , then only you can get the full text articles. But you can read the abstract of each article in free. Basic information of some of important database (Paid and Open Access) is given below.

Proquest

ProQuest Databsase is an online and subscription based database that caters the needs of researcher from the discipline accounting, career and technical education, applied and general science, business, computers, social sciences, telecommunication, trade and industry, arts, humanities, religious periodicals and general interest. It provides, abstracts, full text up to some extent, graphics and images in Adobe Acrobat. It provides, books, videos and audios, dissertations and thesis and also provides a look up for 17 other resources. Following Figure shows this look up:

You can select any one from above list or multiple resources also. You can also have an option to select articles for specific period of time or time range. Individual researcher can get access through his school, library or company. After logging in with your institution's credentials, you will be able to use browse and advanced search option. In advance search , ProQuest offers seven **Look ups** or **browsable indexes**, so you can easily find spelling or format variations of, for example, an author's name or a journal title. You can find the Look up links in the advanced search page and they are available for the following searchable fields: **author**, **publication**, **subject**, **company/organization**, and **person**, **location**. For a description of these fields, please see the **searchable fields table** to the right. Advanced search also provides to create a structured query and searching across different fields using Boolean operators.

Emerald Insight

Emerald Insight is an online and subscription based database which provides seamless access to high-quality, impactful journals, books, case studies, Expert Briefings and a growing collection of open access content to a global audience. Emerald Insight provides abstracts and full text articles from academic journals covering the subject areas of marketing, management, human resources, commercial music, quality, economics, information management, operations, engineering, production and property, education, health and social care. This is very easy to use platform. User can easily search with their keywords or can browse also. All content is presented side-by-side through a predictable interface with intuitive navigation for fast and easy exploration. Emerald Insight provides high-quality journal articles about accounting & finance, marketing, management, human resources, quality, economics, information management, operations, engineering, production and property, education, health and social care and Case studies. Users do not have access to everything on Emerald Insight. If you only want to find full PDFs, run your search and click 'Only content I have access to' on the right-hand side of the results page. It provides search by title, author, keyword, ISBN and DOI. In advance search, you can limit or broaden your search by selecting appropriate resources provided by Emerald Insight. You can also search in a time range. It has the provision of saving search for future reference, if required. Like ProQuest, it also provides open access to limited number of journal articles.

ScienceDirect is a subscription based online database that provides access more than 4000 academic journals and 30, 000 e books published by Elsevier. The metadata and abstracts are free to aces but full text requires subscription.   The journals are categorized under 4 distinct sections:

- Physical Science and Engineering

- Life Science

- Health Sciences

- Social Sciences and Humanities

Search Platform is very simple and provides multiple fields for comprehensive search in advanced search. It also provides open access to 1.4 Million articles.

Web of Science

Web of Science provides access to several literature search database. The main objective is to support scientific and scholarly research.

The Web of Science facilitates a common search language, navigation environment, and data structure which helps researcher to make their search broad across disparate resources.

Web of Science Core Collection contains 21,000 peer-reviewed scholarly journals also more than 205000 conference proceedings and more than 104000 editorily selected books

It enables search across all databases which is useful tp find content in various disciplines, varied document types, and formats. It also helps to discover the citation connections between these diverse content sets.

EBSCO Database

- EBSCO database serves both new and experienced researchers with a variety of features to refine search results. Following are the main features of EBSCO Database.

- Reliable, peer-reviewed content

- Citation assistance

Ability to save searches and results.

- Sophisticated Search

- Direct Access to Full Text

- Intuitive Interface

- Superior Integrations
- Exceptional Support

ERIC Database

The Education Resources Information Center (ERIC) is considered as an online library of education research and information. Institute of Education Sciences from United States Depart of Education sponsors the ERIC. ERIC provides comprehensive, searchable, easy to use , internet based full-text and bibliographic database of education research and information. Which is essential for researcher in education to improve their teaching-learning process and decision making in education.,

ERIC contains 1.5 million bibliographic records of journal articles and other education-related materials, It also contains a good collection of full text gray literature in education.

ERIC provides the Thesaurus of ERIC Descriptors to facilitate users with controlled vocabulary.

IEEE Database

The IEEE Xplore Digital Library database provides access to articles from peer reviewed journals, conference papers in the field of engineering. It provides access to more than 5 million documents related to engineering. The Basic Search tool provides various metadata fields such as title. Abstract, subject, author and keywords.

Academic Search Complete

It is a scholarly, multi-disciplinary database which provides indexes and abstracts for journals and other publications. It contains full-text access to peer-reviewed journals, indexes and abstracts for magazines, monographs, reports, and conference proceedings. The database features some PDF content going back as far as 1867, with the majority of full text titles in searchable PDF format.

Shodhgangotri: It is an Indian repository of research in progress. It halps us to know the ongoing research at various levels. It provides an access to synopsis of Ph.D approved by concerned university authorities. Along with Synopsis of Ph.D, it also provides synopsis of Minir/ major Research Projects and Emeritus Fellowship. From this repository, we get information about current trends and directions of research being conducted in Indian Universities. It also servs as a tool to avoid duplication of research

Shodhganga: It is a reservoir of Indian theses contains theses and dissertations submitted to Indian universities.it is maintained by Information and Library Network (INFLIBNET) Centre – an autonomous Inter-University Centre of the University Grants Commission (UGC) of India. Users can have access to thesis and dissertations submitted by many Indian Universities. Total 544 universities in India have signed MoUs with the INFLIBNET Centre to participate in this project. It is an open access database and provides full text of any thesis and dissertation available on it.

Open access Thesis and Dissertations

Open Access Thesis and Dissertation is a repository of thesis and dissertations submitted to worldwide universities. It helps to find open access thesis and dissertation published around the world. It indexes around 2960883 thesis and dissertations.

JSTOR

JSTOR means Journal Storage provides open access academic content across various formats and disciplines. The collections include top peer-reviewed scholarly journals as well as respected literary journals, academic monographs, research reports from trusted institutes, and diverse primary sources. It provides an access to full text of more than 2,300 journals from 1,000 publishers, with publication dates ranging from 1665 to 2023 (for certain titles). It provides an access to articles in journals in more than 60 disciplines. It also provides access to 1000000 ebooks published by academic publishers. JSTOR now features audio content with searchable transcripts for spoken word content.

- **JSTOR Shared Collections** (previously Open Community Collections) - JSTOR Shared Collections are images and primary sources from the special collections of libraries, museums, and archives around the world.

- **Open Access Books** - 7,800+ Open Access ebooks from 90 publishers, including Brill, Cornell University Press, De Gruyter, and University of California Press.

- **Open Access Journals** - Our growing collection of Open Access journals cover topical areas in sustainability and security studies, and offer broad coverage in the humanities, social sciences, and sciences.

- **JSTOR's Early Journal Content (EJC)** - This content includes journals published prior to the last 95 years in the United States, or prior to the last 143 years if initially published internationally.

- **Research Reports** - More than 39,000 research reports from over 140 policy institutes around the world are freely accessible to everyone on JSTOR. The open research reports are discoverable alongside journals, books, and primary sources, and are clearly labelled as their own content type. We continually add reports as they become available.

Directory of Open Access Journals

Directory of Open Access Jpurnals i.e. DOAJ provides an open access to a large number of journals. Currently it provides access to 18650 open access journals and 8265272 articles from all the areas of science, technology, social sciencesm medicines and humanities.

CHAPTER 5

SEARCHING THE LITERATURE

Previously Literature review was a lengthy task. Researchers used to visit various libraries across the country to collect literature. For research published at international level we need to rely upon the international publications and that too, subscribed. But now days, everything is not on our finger tips. Due to advent of Information and Communication Technology, you can access any kind of research conducted at any level and published anywhere across the world. So there is not limitation to access the literature as nearly all literature is available in digital form on virtual platform. Still many researchers could not access it as they do not know how to access it, how to search it. So as researchers, we must also know the search places and search techniques so as to search access and review a wide range of literature in the field.

There is a very large number of journal publishing research. A large number of thesis and dissertations are also available on internet. We do not know all the journals and thesis or dissertations. So as usual we take the help of Google. But what is Google, many of us do not know that Google is a search engine. Like Google, there are other search engines which can help to search the literature more effectively and more precisely.

Search Engine is a program that helps to search the internet resources containing users' . We have the misconception that search engine provides the information as per our requirement. It actually provides the list of web sites that contains the information that matches your requirement. It is a program that receives your search request, compares it to the entries in the index, and returns results to you . There are differences in the ways various search engines work, but they all perform three basic tasks:

- They search the Internet or select pieces of the information based on important words.

- They keep an index of the words they find

- They allow users to look for words or combinations of words found in that index.

Working of Search Engine

Search Engine performs two major functions:[ii]

1. Crawling and Building an index

2. Providing answers by calculating relevancy & results.

1. Crawling and Building an Index

Search engine crawl on the network of world wide web like a spider and indexes the web pages as well as files in Portable Document Format, JPG, news, videos and media files on the world wide web. Once search engines find these pages, it decipher the code from them and store selected pieces in massive hard drive in data centers of respective search engine. For collecting and storing this abundant information, search engines have constructed data centers all over the world.

The above illustration is described in the following flow figure.

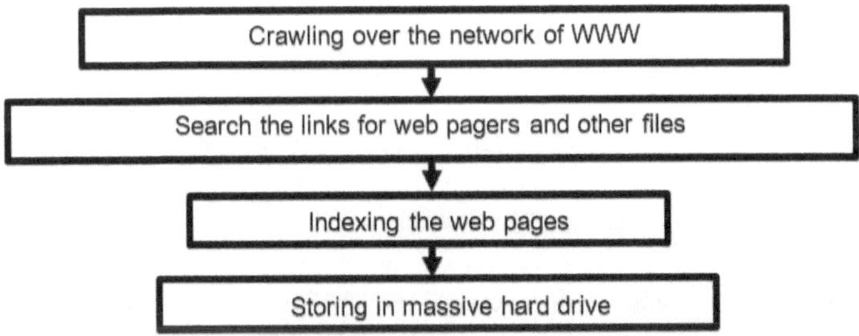

2. Providing answers by calculating relevancy & results

When a user submit a search query to search engines, they search the pages containing the words in user's search query in its database and returns the relevant results.

Search engines are expected to perform two things

1. To return only those results which are relevant to users' requirement

2. Rank those results in order of perceived usefulness.

In short, search engines simply find a page with right words as typed in your search query and returns in appropriate order.

Types of Search Engines

There are five main types of search engines.

1. Web Search Engines

2. Meta Search Engines

3. Federated Search Engines

4. Invisible Web Search Engines

5. Specific Search Engines

    i. Subject specific search engines

    ii. Format specific search engines

Meta Search Engine

Search engines have certain limitations. No search engine can search all the information. The results found through Google may not find through Yahoo or MSN. For comprehensive search you need to search multiple search engines and it consumes time and energy. Meta Search Engine is the solution. In simple words, Meta search engines search the users' information through other search engine. It can be called as "Single Window System". It transmits user's keywords simultaneously to various individual search engines to actually carry out the search. These search engines carry out the search in their databases and return the relevant results to Meta search engines. Then meta search engine collects the results received from various search engines associated with it , integrates all the results, eliminates the duplicate results, adds additional features like clustering and returns the relevant results. The Example of Meta Search Engine is Dogpile, Metacrawler, Mamma. Dogpile is associated with Google, Yahoo and Yandex, It saves time as users need not use various search engines for information searching. Though meta search engine provides you're a broader scope for your search, the results may not always better. Often, the results returned by a meta search engine are not as relevant as those returned by a standard search engine.

Federated Search Engine

Federated search engine performs the federated search. Federated Search means searching over distributed and gheterogenous data sets and providing a unified search results. However, federated search techniques does not provide results from only web but also across various database. Federated search helps us to search case law, court documents, newspaper articles , public records etc. and in return, receive merged results from heterogeneous sources techniques. In simple words, in federated search systems, the task is to search a group of independent collections, and to effectively merge the results they return for queries.

Federated search has two distinct approaches.

1. Query Time Merging.
2. Index Time Merging

1. Query Time Merging : It is faster and easier solution

A query federator intercepts the query, and passes it to multiple search engines. The federator then waits to hear replies from the search engines, and when received, merges or concatenates the results into a results list. This model relies on data repositories to provide a search function.

2. Index Time Merging

This approach requires content to be acquired into a central index, and it is typical of traditional enterprise search systems.

Most search engines default to ranking by relevancy, which is what most users expect. Through acquiring all data into a central index, sophisticated query enhancement and relevancy algorithms can be applied, providing the user with excellent search results.

The Pro Quest and Google Scholar are the best examples of federated search engines.

Invisible Web Search Engine

The term "invisible Web" or "Deep Web" mainly refers to the vast repository of information that general search engines and directories don't have direct access to, like databases. Information in these databases is generally inaccessible to the software spiders and crawlers that create search engine indexes. This invisible web content is estimated to be about 500 times more than what today's search engines can see. Hidden within the pages of these databases lie terabytes of information that is crucial to your day-to-day decision-making. To get at this information, or even to determine if it is pertinent to your subject, you might spend endless hours in manual searching. This is both time-consuming and prone to human error. These invisible or deep webs can be searched through special search engines called as invisible web search engine. Invisible Web search engines are built to construct queries, which connect with dynamic content in real- time in order to obtain current information. Since the types of queries vary widely depending on the type of database being queried, invisible web search applications are focused on searching pre-selected data sources where the search intent and underlying content are known. This has led to the use of invisible web search technology in building "Vertical Searches" or "specialized searches" that focus on specific businesses. The good examples of invisible search engines are www.Scirus.com , Thevirtuallibrary.com, www.invisibleweb.com, www.completeplanet.com and www.vlib.org.

Specific Search Engines

These are domain specific search engines. For searching information in different subject these specific search engines can be used. There are two types of these specific search engines.

1. Subject specific search engines

2. Format specific search engine.

Subject specific search engines intends to search the information in specific subject. For example. Scirus for science, History Engine for History, Mathguide for Mathematics, Geosearchengine for Geogaphy. As these search engines index the pages only in their specialized field, the chances of getting relevant results than general search engines is always high.

For different format of information, format specific search engines are more helpful. For example for pictures picsearch, tubesurf for videos, findsounds for sounds etc.

Subject Gateways

Subject gateways are specialized catalogues in which the information has been selected and organized by a person or an organization. Subject gateways are built up hierarchically; you can choose from a number of sub-categories within each subject in order to limit your search results.

Aim of a subject gateway is to help users in locating relevant and high quality resources on the Internet. A subject gateways is an online librarian which locates online resources what librarians do for books" Unlike search engines, subjects gateways are built by humans and it contains selected information about a specific subject. There are various subject gateways for various disciplines.

• Medicine	OMNI
• Engineering	EEVL
• Art	ADAM
• Social Science	SOSIG
• Business	Biz/ed
• History	History
• General	BUBL/NISS

Web Portals

Portals are the websites that serves as a gateway or a main entry point ('cyber door') on the internet to a specific field-of-interest or an industry. A portal provides at least four essential services:

1. search engine(s),
2. email,
3. links to other related sites, and
4. personalized content.

It may also provide facilities such as chat, members list, free downloads, etc. Portals such as AOL, MSN, Net center, and Yahoo, earn their revenue from membership fees and/or by selling advertising space on their web pages also called portal site or web portal. While there are

Jaykar Library of University of Pune has its own portal i.e Jaykar Library Portal from where you can access the journal database/s those subscribed by Jaykar Library.

Now it is a usual practice to search any information on internet. We are now more used to with internet than books and other printed material. When we think to search something new, out fingers start working and we log on to Google or any other search engine. We insert our query, which is in the form of statement or general terms in natural language. But what we find? Do we get satisfied with the results obtained from internet? NOT ALWAYS!!!!!. WHY? This is because we are lacking of search strategy and search techniques. We can find information on any subject, discipline in any form or type, but need is to apply systematic strategy and universal techniques. From this module you will learn both of these i.e. strategies and techniques to search the information.

Search Strategy

When you start to search a new information in library catalogue, journal database, internet, it is a good practice to do some intellectual paper work. Before logging into search engines, you first need to get clear idea about your topics, i.e. what the topic interpret, which are the main concept/s and/or term/s? , which are the standard terms? What is the relationship between selected concepts or terms. We go through an example for more understanding.

Suppose you want to search an information on mind mapping. We should follow the following steps.

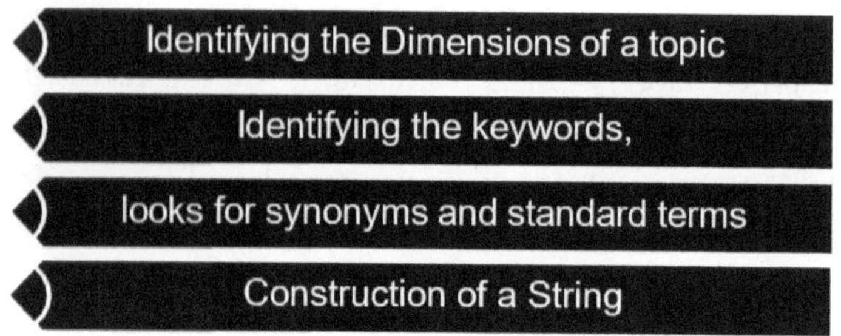

1. Identifying the Dimensions of the topic

- Learning techniques
- Definition of Mind Mapping
- Mind Maps
- Construction/Drawing of Mind Maps
- Benefits of Mind Mapping Technique
- Mind Map Construction Packages

In above list, you can see one dimension "Learning Techniques" which seems to be irrelevant to the topic. But Mind Mapping is one of the learning techniques, somebody may think necessary to get information of all learning techniques and then proceed towards the technique of Mind Mapping. "Learning Techniques" is the broader term under which the narrower term "Mind Mapping" comes. The dimensions can be written in natural language.

2. Identifying the key words

The second step after identifying the dimensions, we need to convert these dimension in keywords as follows.

Key word 1	Key word 1	Key word 1	Key word 1	Key word 1	Key word 1
Learning Techniques	Mind Mapping	Mind Maps	Constru ction/ Drawing	Benefits/ use/ pros and cons	Concept/ Definition

3. Identifying the synonyms

Once we listed the keywords, we need to identify the synonyms for them. In above example in above example mind maps can be constructed or can be drawn or we can search benefits or use or pros and cons of mind mapping which have similar meanings. So we should think more on keywords and their synonyms. For this purpose we can use Thesaurus or its online version thesaurus. com. In some cases, the information is indexed under standard terms for example, in an education disciples we use the word Adolescents instead of Teen agers, or use Elementary Education instead of Primary Education. So we also think about the standard terms which are practiced in specific discipline.

4. Construction of a String

After listing the keyword, next step is to construct a string by establishing relationship between two or more keyword by using operators.

Take an example of Mind Mapping. We have listed the keywords. From these keywords, following string can be constructed.

- Learning Techniques AND Mind Maps

- Definition AND Mind Mapping

- Benefits AND Mind Mapping

- (Construction OR Drawing) AND Mind Maps

You may think about AND & OR which is used in above string. These are Boolean Operators which help us a lot in searching an information. AND Operator interprets that both the words of either side of AND must be appear in the search results. For example, from first string, you will find only those article which contains both the words learning techniques and mind mapping. In short, by using AND operator, we can narrow down our search. By using OR operator can have broad search. For example in the last string you will get the results which contains construction of mind maps or drawing of mind maps or you can get both of these. More details about these Boolean operators will be studied in the topic "Boolean Search".

Search Techniques

When conducting Internet searches, there are several very useful search techniques for finding the most reliable information available. If you inculcate these techniques, you can search near about 90% appropriate the information. In this module, some basic and usual search techniques are discussed. They are as follows.

- Phrase Search

- Boolean Search

- Truncation Search

- Range Search

- Proximity Search
- Limiting the Search
- Fussy Search

Phrase Searching

A type of search that allows users to search for documents containing an exact sentence or phrase, rather than single keywords. For example, Mind Mapping, it contains two words with different meanings i.e. mind and mapping. If you search by the word Mind Mapping, you will get the documents containing the word mind only or containing the word mapping only or you will also get the documents containing both of these words i.e. Mind Mapping in any sequence. This means you may get more irrelevant results. Instead of typing Mind Mapping only , if you type it in between inverted comma like "Mind Mapping", you will get the documents containing the exact word as Mind Mapping. This will give you more relevant results as compared to previous.

Boolean Search

Boolean Searches allows you to combine words or phrases using the operators "AND", "OR", "NOT" and "NEAR". Use of these operators helps us to limit, widen or define your search. Most of the search engines support the use of Boolean Search.

AND Operator

AND Operator narrows a search by combining two or more terms; It will retrieve only those documents that contains all the specified terms .

"Elementary Education" AND "Secondary Education".

This search string will retrieve only those documents that contains both the terms i.e. elementary education and secondary education. You can use + sign instead of writing AND.

OR Operator

OR Operator broadens a search by retrieving the documents contains either of two or more words or all the specified words.

"Elementary Education" OR "Secondary Education".

This search string will retrieve the documents containing either of these two words or the documents containing both the words.

NOT Operator

NOT Operator narrows a search by excluding specified search terms. "Elementary Education in India" NOT Maharashtra.

This search string will retrieve the documents containing the information about elementary education in India excluding the elementary education in Maharashtra.

Truncation Search

Truncation searching allows you to retrieve documents containing variations on a search term. During this search, type the first few letters of the keyword followed by an asterisk (*).

Creat* this string will retrieve the documents containing the words create, creation, creation, creating etc.

Similarly Color* : coloring, color, colored etc.

Proximity Search

Proximity searching enables you to search based on where, and how close, two or more search terms appear in the search result. Search engines and databases utilize a variety of different proximity operators.

WRT Operator

Suppose as an education students you need to find the information about working of brain. If you insert a string like "working of Brain", you will retrieve the documents containing the information about working of brain, but it may be related to Zoology or Medicine or Psychology. You want to search in information of brain from education point of view, then you need to use WRT Operator.

"Working of Brain" **WRT** Education. Here WRT means With Respect To. "Problems of Adolescents" **WRT** "Health Education".

NEAR Operator

It Searches for terms near each other. For example you want to search the documents containing the the two terms "problems" and "education " with certain distance. You can specify it as

"Problem" **NEAR** "Education". Search engine will yield the results only when these two are within certain distance.

Sentence/Phrase Operator

It Searches for terms in same section of result in sentence, paragraph, etc. You can specify it as

"Napoleon" SENTENCE "France": search engine or database will yield results where "Napoleon" and "France" are in the same sentence or you can specify

"Napoleon" PARAGRAPH "France": search engine or database will yield results where "Napoleon" and "France" are in the same paragraph.

Fussy Search

A fuzzy search is a process that locates Web pages that are likely to be relevant to a search argument even when the argument does not exactly correspond to the desired information. A fuzzy search is done by means of a fuzzy matching program, which returns a list of results based on likely relevance even though search argument words and spellings may not exactly match. Exact and highly relevant matches appear near the top of the list. Subjective relevance ratings, usually as percentages, may be given. If you retrieving an information about "Portuguese" and if you entered this word with wrong spelling i.e. portuguse, then search engine will ask you "Did you mean Portuguese". Alternative spellings, and words that sound the same but are spelled differently, are given. More, if you enter the word "information", search engine.

Range Search

While searching an information about specific product you can specify the numeric range. For example, if you want to purchase digital camera and you budget is Rs. 5000-7000. You can specify it by using range searching.

"Digital Camera"..Rs. 5000..Rs. 7000.

By using this range search, you can get results containing the information of digital cameras ranging in between Rs. 5000 to Rs. 7000 only.

More Examples:

Dumbbells ..10KG..20KG

"Places around Pune" ..10km..20km

Limiting the Search

You can limit your search by using this search techniques. You will understand it from following table.

PDF: "Mind Mapping"	You will get only PDF documents containing information about Mind Mapping. You can also specify DOC, PPT for documents and presentation type files.
DEFINE: "Mind Mapping"	You will get only those documents containing the definitions of Mind Mapping, You can also use BENEFITS, CAUSES, DIMENSIONS etc.
IND: Cricket	You will get only those documents containing information of cricket in India

VIDEO: "Mind Mapping"	You will get only videos on Mind Mapping
IMAGE: "Mind Mapping"	You will get only images on Mind Mapping

CHAPTER 6

EVALUATION OF LITERATURE

We access information from various sources ranging from manuscripts to digital. But we retrieve the information blindly from these sources. Most of us have misconception that the information in a book or found on internet is always right. But it is not always true. The trueness and other quality dimensions of information are strongly depend upon the sources in which it is incorporated. So we need to evaluate the information sources before retrieving the information.

Books and journals are the common and basic sources of information. But they need not to be evaluated because, books are published only after publishers' or editors' review. Before purchasing the books libraries also apply critical evaluation by respective persons in the field. So as a user of the books, we need not evaluate the books. The same case is about journals. Before publishing an article in journal, it has to undergo through the process of peer review or blind review. If it provides some new facts, then only a particular journal publishes that article. As a user, we need not evaluate the journals also. Then, question comes in mind: what to review and why? The answer is WWW.

As we know, information exists on a huge network of World Wide Web. There is no screening or evaluating or reviewing authority on internet. Anyone can create a website or webpage and can put any information on it. When we search the information through search engine, it returns only list of websites/pages those contain relevant information as per out requirement. Search engine do not evaluate the information. So there is a strong need to evaluate the website from where we access the information. There are some basic criterions to evaluate the websites. These are as follows:

Evaluation Criterions	Questions to be asked for specific criterions
Accuracy	• Who wrote the page and can you contact him or her? • What is the purpose of the document and why was it produced? • Is this person qualified to write this document?. • Make sure author provides e-mail or a contact address/phone number. • Know the distinction between author and Webmaster.
Authority	• Who published the document and is it separate from the "Webmaster?" • Check the domain of the document, what institution publishes this document? • Does the publisher list his or her qualifications?

Evaluation Criterions	Questions to be asked for specific criterions
	• What credentials are listed for the authors? • Where is the document published? Check URL domain.
Objectivity	• What goals/objectives does this page meet? • How detailed is the information? • What opinions (if any) are expressed by the author? • Determine if page is a mask for advertising; if so information might be biased. • Ask yourself: why was this written and for whom?
Currency	• When was it produced? • When was it updated? • How up-to-date are the links (if any)? • How many dead links are on the page? • Are the links current or updated regularly? • Is the information on the page outdated?

In short we should ask following eight questions before retrieving the information.

- What can the URL tell you?

- Who wrote the page? Is he, she, or the authoring institution a qualified authority?

- Is it dated? Current, timely?

- Is information cited authentic?

- Does the page have overall integrity and reliability as a source?

- What's the bias?

- Could the page or site be ironic, like a satire or a spoof?

- If you have questions or reservations, how can you satisfy them?

Web site evaluation is an important task. As out decision making and further actions are strongly depend upon the retrieved information , we need to evaluate the sources from where we retrieved the information.

CHAPTER 7

READING THE LITERATURE

Harris, Dave (2020) says "the purpose of reading is to understand what the author has to say. It is to understand the theories an evidence presented." Though it looks like a simple task, it is a very complex task. If you read the literature superficially, you will not come across exactly what the author or researcher wants to say. You may missed out many dimensions. You are supposed to interpret the words, sentences in appropriate manner as each word can have many meanings those could be used in different situations. You need to understand the perspective of an author behind using the specific word, phrase or a sentence. This appropriate interpretation leads you towards better understanding of the work of that researcher or author. You need to understand the exact message that author or researcher wants to convey. If you keep this perspective, as a researcher, you can develop your own scholarly voice based on the available publication. The citations given in a literature also matters a lot. It helps us to understand how the particular author sees towards the research community in the area. What are the dimensions of the areas about which the researchers are thinking. What are different perspectives of reserchers across the world towards a particular area. This helps us to widen our perspective towards research community and helps us to develop our own perspective with proper justification. With reading scholarly literature, you main aim is to relate the literature with your own research. You need to understand whether any new theory, model or standard is introduced, whether old theories, models or standards are criticized and /or revised. Reading the literature develops your thinking and widen your perspectives towards various dimensions of research methodology used in different conditions in the area. It helps you to take proper decision related to selection of research design, developing research tool, using appropriate statistical techniques etc.

Your aim towards reading a literature is also important. If you want to make your research better than what is available, you are supposed to read the best of the literature available. If you are accepting everything published and you think that there is not more scope to take this further, then you could never develop your own idea and perspective. If you accept each new piece as equally valuable, and that your own ideas and work as a scholar can make a worthy contribution to your field, Harris (2020).

If you want to raise your scholarly voice, you need to disclose the lacking areas of available theories, the dimensions of subject or entire subject that is not covered so far, any lacuna or error in theory. This all is called as a "gap" in terms of research. You can grow your scholarship by showing and justifying the gaps in available literature. This gaps should not be superficial it should be serious gaps and that too with proper justifications and possible solutions through your research. Finding gaps is not so easy, for this you need to have evaluative intention while reading. If you are agreeing with everything in the literature, you will not be able to develop yourself as a researcher. You should have something challenging attitude and always keep yourself in the state of questioning that, why this is so? What could happened if this was done in some different way? Why he would have not tried or used this research tool? Is is really feasible in the current condition? And like that. This questioning will lead you to get new perspectives that the author or researcher.

While reading the literature, always keep your research in your mind. At every stage you may need to define or refine your research. As your reading goes on, you may need to rethink of your Design, tools, techniques, population, scope etc. You may agree or disagree with the ideas, you may completely reject the idea, you may find any innovative or new ideas that has not been introduced previously. This all should come up with proper and logical justification in terms of your research. This thankful reading leads you towards the better understanding of the area and research methodology. With thinkful reading you can develop your research attitude, critical thinking ability and obviously your understandings.

Next question which is generally asked by researcher that how much literature should I read? The answer is very simple. You read the literature until you get the satisfied answers to your all questions. There is not specific number of articles or thesis or dissertation to read. It also cannot be said that this amount of literature is enough. The literature should build your foundation on which your entire research could be developed. There should not be doubt about what and why you are doing in your research. Your scholarly voice should be come out of the literature. Secondly, your main objective is not the literature review. Mind that, literature review is one of the dimensions or step in your research. Agreed that it is important, but if you spend much time on this, your future steps in research may get affected. You cannot allocate sufficient time for further research. So there is no specific number of articles or thesis or dissertations to read and no specific time to be allocated for it. In a simple way, you keep reading right from the point that you encounter a problem till finalizing your findings.

Next issue that many research could faced that there are many definitions of a particular concept. All the definitions are accepted and seems reliable. Which definition should be accepted for the project? In this case you are supposed to study all the available definitions from your research point of view. For each definition you should write your own justification regarding whether it is suitable for your research or not. On the other hand after citing all the definitions, you can define your own definition in terms of your research if the available definitions can not fulfill your requirement. E.g. there are around 30 definitions of a concept "information literacy". After studying and citing all the definitionsdefinied by various reliable and authorized organizations and scholars right from 1970 till 2015 , it came to notice that a point "cyber security" is missing from all the definitions. So while summing up this dimensions, a researcher came up with modified definition of information literacy including a new dimension as "accessing information securely".

Breaking down the literature in various dimensions will minimize the complexity of the literature. You are supposed to break down your research topic into various dimensions and should search and read the literature according to the dimensions. This will serve two purposes first, it will ease the process of literature review and second, you will not miss any dimension of the research topic.

e.g. Research Title is "Developing Information Literacy Programme for students of Pre service Teacher Education : An Experimental Research."

The area of research is Information Literacy. So the topic is broken down in following dimensions according to the research topic.

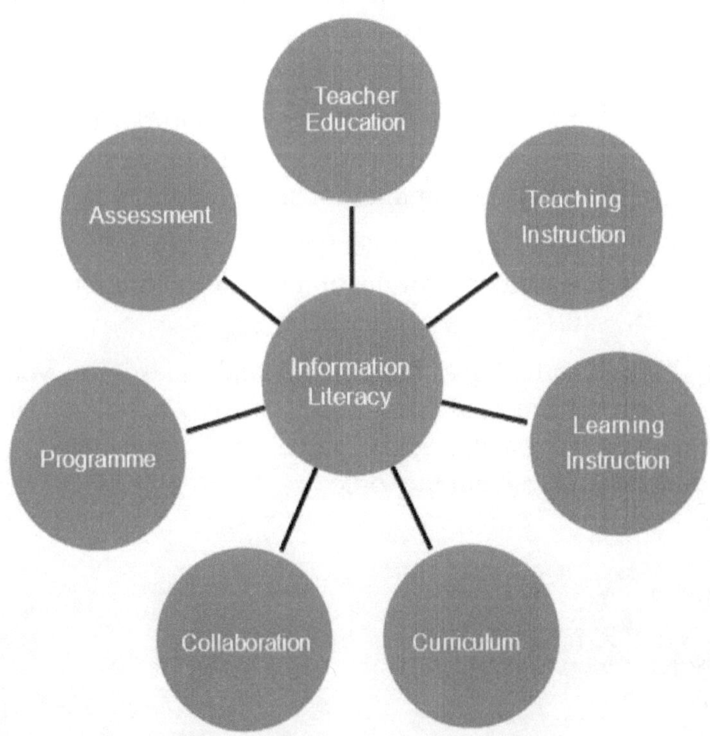

After breaking down the topic in various dimensions, automatically the questions are also formed as:

1. Which teaching instructions have been practiced while teaching information literacy?

2. Which learning instructions have been practiced while teaching information literacy?

3. Are there any developed curriculums or are there any guidelines to develop information literacy curriculum?

4. Can information literacy programmed be developed, planned and implemented in collaboration between librarian and teachers?

5. Which organizations or institutions have developed and implementing various information literacy programmes for teacher education?

6. Which methods or tools are practiced in assessment or evaluation of information literacy skills?

Based on above dimensions and questions, you can search and read literature dimension wise. So that you can have a multidimensional and comprehensive understanding about the topic.

CHAPTER 8

WRITING A REVIEW

What you did till reach up to this step? You decided your topic, accordingly broke down it in various dimensions, search literature from various sources using appropriate search strategy and search techniques, accessed the literature, read deeply for understanding and now you are in the state of writing the review. Your literature review is reflection of your understanding about the topic. It reflects the scope of the research. It communicates the scholarly work that has been carried out previous to your research and what is your perspective towards it. It clearly shows the gaps in the area. So in that sense, your critical thinking is reflected in your writing.

It is not advisable to write complete review after reading the complete literature. You should write side by along with reading also. If you are reading literature dimension wise, start writing review about that dimension at the same time. You are supposed to decide the sequence of writing i.e. whether to write chronologically, whether to write conceptually etc. In case of definitions, it is advisable to write the definitions chronologically right from first definition when the term for the concept was coined till the latest definition, as it specifies the conceptual journey of the concept. You will get clear idea about the progress of the concept across the time. Many dimensions of topic can evolve across the time so, you can take decision whether to write the review chronologically for all the dimensions or not.

Use literature because it helps you tell your own story. Write about literature to provide comparison to your own work and ideas. This is directly parallel to the attitude needed for reading, Harris (2020). You are using the literature as a tool to tell your research story. Many times, researcher tell more about what other researches have done so far and less about their own research or gaps. Instead you are supposed to demonstrate your understanding from your research point of view based on the literature. After reading your literature review, a reader should get the clear idea about your research.

The purpose should also be clearly mentioned. What you are seeking from the literature should be clearly written. i.e. if you are writing a review about assessment in information literacy, you should clearly write the purposes as follows:

1. To review various types of assessment or evaluation for information literacy

2. To review various tools that were developed, used and tested for assessment or evaluation of information literacy skills.

3. To review the available standardized tools for assessment or evaluation of information literacy.

These purposes demonstrate your understanding about the dimension "Assessment or Evaluation of Information Literacy Skills". Writing these purposes also useful for you to keep your review limited.

While writing a review, you are supposed to make justifiable arguments. Because main purpose of the literature review is not the summarizing of previous studies. Rather it aims to demonstrate your scholarly voice, your different perspective towards the area of research. It's a critical evaluation and not the commentary. It is not others research story that you are telling, it is your own research story that gives a foundation to your research. So the text that you are supposed to use while writing should be an argumentative text and not the narrative. It's not a narration, it's sequential arguments with proper justification, evidences and logic.

The length of the review is also a debatable issue. Who long should be y review? It depends on "what you want to say?" There is no specific length, rather it should clearly focuses on the purpose. It should cover all the predefined dimensions. It should not be too lengthy or too short. It should clearly and comprehensively communicate your scholarly voice. It should reflect your understanding about the topic.

The language you are using is also a tool. You are not supposed to use the same language as in literature. The language should be simple and communicative. The confusing words or sentences should be avoided. A reader of your review can clearly interpret about what your are saying. A lengthy or flowery words and sentences should be avoided. It is not an essay in essay writing competitions, it's a mature writings, so your language plays an important role. Though your are not agreed with the arguments, you are supposed to given justification in proper and communicative language. The connectors like, secondly, on the other hand, across the times etc. should be used effectively so that continuity can be maintained. Below is an example of how we can write review in a simple language.

Information Literacy and Teacher Education

This dimension covers the surveys and other research expressing the need and facts about information literacy skills for pre-service and in service teachers.

Though the concept of information literacy was evolved in 1974, roots of this concept could be found in 19th century in terms of library instructions. The need for library instructions was first identified by Emma Adams in 1898. She surveyed twenty "foremost" normal schools and found that 19 out of 20 schools were providing library instructions in various forms like formal instructions, library class, assignments etc. (Adams, 1898). In 1915 the National Education Association (NEA) conducted a survey of 100 school supervisors to determine what knowledge a teacher should have about libraries. After analyzing results, the committee recommended a standard courserequired for the use of the library for all normal school students along with a lengthier course in directing children's reading and an optional course in library organization and administration to prepare teacher librarians (NEA, 1915). Harris (1934) summarized above researches to ascertain the status of library instructions for teachers at that time using the catalogues of 114 accredited state teachers' colleges as her source. She proposed that teacher education students complete an advanced bibliography course to provide practice in research techniques. She also presented a sample curriculum for a model programme. She recommended an introductory bibliography course focused on learning about reference sources along with children literature course. Garber (1954), a public librarian, presented anecdotal evidence to demonstrate that the teacher's lack of library skills leads to construction of inappropriate and frustrating assignments for pupils. Saddler (1970) reported a study of information presented about libraries in Kentucky teacher-training programmes to assess the attitudes conveyed by instructional materials and the accuracy of information presented. She found that while almost three-fourths of the institutions responding had formal library instruction programs for education graduate students, only one fourth taught a unit on the library as a part of the undergraduate education curriculum. O'Hanlon (1987) surveyed faculty in Ohio elementary teacher–training programs to assess attitudes towards library instructions in teacher training curriculum and towards the role of elementary school teacher in library skills development of pupils. All the respondents strongly supported the provision of library instructions for teacher trainees. Respondents also indicated that elementary school teachers should play an important role in fostering information skills in pupils. Half of the respondents reported that current graduates of their teacher training programmes were inadequately prepared to assume this role. O'Hanlon(1988,528)conducted a historical analysis of articles and documents (published between 1904 & 1987) that described "continuing efforts by academic librarians in United States to promote library instructions in teacher education programmes and found that the academic librarians have attempted to convince teacher educators of the value of bibliographic instructions for more than 80 years without much success". She further suggested that "library literate teachers, working cooperatively with school library personnel could ensure successful resource based instructional programmes that simultaneously strengthen their students' library research skills, critical thinking abilities, and problem solving skills".

From above literature, it can be understood that teacher-training institutes were not much keen towards providing effective library instructions. They were satisfied only in providing library orientations or some library periods or some library classes. All the authors up to 1988 strongly expressed the need of standardized format of library instruction in teacher training course.

It should not look like a monotonous story, it should take the reader further along with its journey and at the end reader should realize your own story telling the gaps. You can use different verbs while giving evidences Below is an example that shows who to make connections and maintaining continuity.

In 1998, the Association of College and Research Libraries (ACRL) **issued** "A progress Report on Information literacy". This report updated the findings of the ALA Presidential Committee on Information literacy (1989) and described progress made towards implementing the committee's recommendations. **The ACRL reported** that teacher education programmes had made no real progress in modifying course requirements and performance expectations to addressinformation literacy concerns (ACRL, 2000). **Johnson and O'English (2003) compiled** an annotated bibliography of articles on information literacy education in the United States and

Canada published since 1980s.They noted that successful and innovative programmes where exposure to librarians , integration of IL instructions, and attentions to library research can produce new information literate teachers who are equipped to collaborate with school librarians and teach information literacy and research skills to their students. **Usluel (2007) conducted a survey** with 1702 students in Turkey teachers using the information literacy self- efficacy scale and duration of ICT usage. The results showed that student teachers level of self-efficacy and duration of ICT usage were determining factors for information literacy and self- efficacy. He strongly stated that training during university education has an important role in increasing information literacy and self-efficacy. **Wen and Shin (2008) carried out a study** to establish information literacy competency standards for elementary and high schoolteachers in Taiwan. The process included a set of two expert round table discussion and three rounds of Delphi technique survey. The study found that the dimension "attitude" is the most powerful force for promoting teachers' information literacy competence and their willingness to apply information   technology in teaching. Authors also suggested the proposed standards, hope that it could serve as a self-evaluation tool for teachers as well as the basis for staffing and training programmes for elementary, and highschool teachers in Taiwan. **Probert (2008) surveyed 138 teachers** from 3 school in New Zealand in order to investigate teachers' understanding of informationliteracy and their associated classroom practices. In finding, she reported that while some of the teachers in the project had a reasonably good understanding of the concept of information literacy, very few reported developing their students' information literacy skills. **Duke and Ward (2009) conducted a meta synthesis** of the literature available on information literacy instructions in teacher training.

Writing conclusion is the last step of your literature review. The conclusion summarizes the main ideas of all the dimensions and demonstrates your own criticism on it. It shows the exact gaps in the literature. It comments on the facts should express the need of your current research. It shows the journey of entire literature review process and also gives an idea of sources you consulted. It does not show only gaps, but it also shows the things that motivate you, that inspire you to conduct your research. It does not say "nothing has happened" or "Nothing is to be happened". It says "This has been happened and this is to be done in this manner". It is argumentative as

well as expository so as to expose the previous research. The conclusion should make your research more factual, logical and justifiable. Greetham (2021) says that the success of literature review depends upon two things. First, it should be written clearly and concisely in a style that is simple to understand and interesting to read. Second, there should be a clear rational behind the literature you have chosen and planned to use-it should make coherent sense. Following is an example of a concluding a Literature Review.

A number of research papers and conceptual papers on various dimensions of information literacy programmes were studied for writing this research. Almost all the research work was carried out in countries other than India. Very few conceptual papers written by Indian Authors have found so far. Many research papers on various dimensions of information literacy i.e. teaching of information literacy, learning of information literacy, collaboration in information literacy programmes, integration of information literacy with curriculum have studied. In Indian scenario except Delhi University and recently the proposed project of information literacy by Kendriya Vidyalaya, none of the university or organization has developed information literacy programmes. In Many Indian Universities, doctoral researches is information literacy are ongoing but not published.

Through the literature review, it is revealed that the relation between information literacy and Teacher Education established since 1934 in terms of library skills. Much research has been carried out in the field of teacher education about information literacy. The Information literacy skills assessment, information literacy programmes are developed and implemented for elementary, secondary and higher education teachers and teacher education students-both pre service and in-service. It is globally accepted fact that there is a strong need to impart information literacy skills within teachers so that they can play an important role in fostering information literacy skills in pupils. Most of the information literacy programmes are integrated with teacher education curriculum and give strong emphasis on teacher and librarian collaboration for planning, developing, implementing and evaluating the information literacy programme. Most of the leading teacher education institutions have carried out case studies, surveys and programmes on information literacy. Specialized information literacy tests have been developed for teacher education students. ACRL has developed specialized Information literacy Competency Standards for Teacher Education. More attention is paid towards the library or information skills for teachers globally. Many foreign universities have developed a variety of information literacy programmes and applied new approaches in implementing those programmes. A variety of tutorials in both versions i.e. prints and online is available especially for teacher education. Stand alone course, introductory course, integrated course, summer courses have been developed by many universities and institutions collaboratively by librarians and faculty in the field of teacher education. Various researchers, professional organizations have expressed the need of information literacy education in teacher training course. Various researches also supported the same. But from above literature and researcher's experience, it is revealed that still there is tremendous scope for imparting information literacy in teacher training courses. Though various teacher educators and library professionals have researched many dimensions and strongly expressed the need, developed models, standards and programmes for teacher education, information literacy is not unanimously accepted as a natural dimension of teacher training. In Indian scenario, no evidence of research on information literacy tied with teacher education was found in the literature.

At international level governments and educational organizations, associations are giving planned emphasis on information literacy skills for teachers. As these all initiatives are being taken at global level, in India we have the clean slate regarding information literacy and teacher education. None of the Indian Universities or institutions, educational organization or association and policy makers except Knowledge Commission of India has taken initiatives in fostering information literacy to teachers. The present research is an effort in developing and implementing a need-based information literacy programme for the students of pre-service teacher education during their pre-service teacher training.

Through the literature available on information literacy instruction, it is revealed that the emphasis is given on instruction creatively. Teaching information literacy to students does not mean to make them orient about library services and bibliographic instructions. It includes variety of instructional approaches like course related library instruction sessions, course integrated projects, online tutorials and standalone courses. Various instructional methods or techniques have been applied in teaching information literacy skills viz. Cephalonia method, personal response system, group work exercise, application of Bloom's Taxonomy, POGIL technique, unit based instruction, inquiry teaching, instruction by using games and short story, use of workbook, graphic organizers. With the creative methods and techniques and web 2.0 instructions are also applied in various information literacy instruction sessions like online tutorial, web based games, CAI programmes, use of multimedia etc. After deep study of above literature it can be stated that there is no standard approach or method recommended unanimously. Though various approaches and methods were used by researches, all these methods have certain limitation related to education system, level of students and infrastructure. After deep study of information literacy instruction, researcher would like to state that the nature, approach and type of instruction should be based on the educational system and students' understanding level. In the present research, short story, game, demonstration and of course lectures were used. The handbook created in the present research was made available to all student teachers through their mail. Majority of the sessions were technology based sessions, which included power point slide show and demonstration through internet.

Through Literature review on learning, itis revealed that much literature is available on explaining relationship between learning and information literacy and that there is a strong connection between learning and informationliteracy. The emphasis is given upon use of learning theories, various learning styles and various learning techniques. Various learning techniques have been used so far e.g. learning management system, gaming, and self directed learning, printed as well as online tutorial, comparing and evaluating information sources etc. more it is strongly recommended that the information literacy learning should be based on one of the learning theories and appropriate learning style should be applied. Through above literature it could be stated that a equal emphasis is given on learning. Various learning approaches have been used. But as information literacy is related to cognitive skills development, a constructivist approach is mostly used by many researchers. Various learning techniques based on constructivist approach have been used. As like teaching, not one learning technique is effective, learning technique is to be selected based on education system and level of students. In the present research, an emphasis is also given on learning. In order to facilitate student teachers' learning of information literacy, concept mapping and self directed learning techniques were used. Tutorials in the form of handbooks was also created and made it available to all student teaches in both form i.e. hard copy and soft copy.

In case of teacher education in India, the research is not giving even a bit of emphasis on learning in the area of information literacy. However, in the present research an emphasis is given on the learning aspect of information literacy. The tutorial in the form of Information literacy Handbook was distributedfor self-learningin both the form i.e. printedand online form. Self directed learning technique was applied during the practical session of "applying search techniques". Gamewasused for learning evaluation of information and conceptmapping technique was applied for exploring information sources.

In case of literature review on "context" aspect of information literacy, it is revealed that information literacy is not an isolated entity. Like teaching and learning, it is always associated with relevant subject matter and context. Much research is carried out in the information literacy in content with English, Arts, Nursing, Firefighter and Teacher Education. In the context with curriculum, the strong emphasis is given on the integration of information literacy with the curriculum of specific discipline. It is recommended that information literacy programme should be developed in integration with curriculum of specific discipline. Many universities and institutions abroad have integrated their information literacy programme with the curriculum in the discipline like Nursing, Biology, History, English, Computer studies and Teacher Education. In the present research, this curriculum aspect of information literacy is also considered. The present information literacy programme is developed in the context with Teacher Education and based on the classroom teaching learning practices, whichare expected in the B.Ed. curriculum of SavitribaiPhulePune University.

Much literaturewas found on the collaboration aspect of information literacy programme. It is strongly recommended that the collaboration have greater impact on the success of information literacy programmes. Literature has emphasized on the collaboration between librarian and faculty, libraries of two different universities, library and a university department. Also various levels of collaboration were explained in literature. Without participation of manpower in whole institution, i.e. right from policy maker to classroom teacher, everyone should work collaboratively in planning and designing information literacy programme, deciding topics to be included, deciding instructional methods, organizing classroom instructional session, creating tutorials and making critical evaluation of Information literacy skills of students.

Regarding information literacy assessment, various tools and techniques have been used viz. case studies, rubrics, portfolios, action research and various information literacy standards. Along with these tools few professional tools also have been used so far like SAILS and ILIAC. In the present research, the assessment of information literacy skills in pre-test and post-test was carried out by using information literacy test for teacher education which is based on ACRL's information Literacy Competency Standards for Teacher Education.

In the present research, all the aspects of information literacy education have been covered. The information literacy programme is based on pre-service teacher education curriculum, and it includes a variety of instructional and learning techniques and according to ACRL Information literacy Competency Standards for Teacher Education. Thus, this is a unique research about information literacy for the students of pre-service teacher education.

So, it could be said that, literature review is not merely a chapter in your thesis or dissertation. It is a process that starts with the research and ends with the research. It is a continuous and systematic process that contribute in your research. It acts a bridge joining the knowledge gap. It justifies your research. It demonstrates your understanding about a topic. It is a story that tells everything about research in a particular field.

REFERENCES

Bem, D. J. (1995). Writing a Review Article for Psychological Bulletin Psychological Bulletin.

Dewey, A. & Drahota, A. (2016) Introduction to systematic reviews: online learning module Cochrane Training, https://training.cochrane.org/interactivelearning/module-1-introduction-conducting-systematic-reviews

Hart, C (1998). Doing a literature Review: Releasing the Social Science Research imagination. Thousand Oaks, CA:Sage.

Fink, A (2005). Conducting Research Literature Reviews: From the internet to Paper, 2nd edn. London: Sage Publication

Moll-Willard, Elizabeth (2019). Literature Review Survival Guide. [PowerPoint slides]. https://www.slideshare.net/ElizabethMoll4/how-to-do-a-literature-review-89998789

Munn, Z., Peters, M. D. J., Stern, C., Tufanaru, C., McArthur, A., & Aromataris, E. (2018). Systematic review or scoping review? Guidance for authors when choosing between a systematic or scoping review approach. BMC *Medical Research Methodology, 18*(1), 143.

Onwuegbuzie, Anthony J. and Frels, Rebecca (2016). Seven Steps to a Comprehensive Literature Review: A Multimodal and Cultural Approach. Sage, New Delhi.